Teaching

Intelligent Design

Essential Viewpoints

Teaching

Intelligent Design

By Hal Marcovitz

Content Consultant
Corrinne Bedecarre, PhD
Instructor of Philosophy
Normandale Community College

ABDO
Publishing Company

CREDITS

Published by ABDO Publishing Company, 8000 West 78th Street, Edina, Minnesota 55439. Copyright © 2010 by Abdo Consulting Group, Inc. International copyrights reserved in all countries. No part of this book may be reproduced in any form without written permission from the publisher. The Essential Library™ is a trademark and logo of ABDO Publishing Company.

Printed in the United States.

Editor: Holly Saari
Copy Editor: Paula Lewis
Interior Design and Production: Emily Love
Cover Design: Emily Love

Library of Congress Cataloging-in-Publication Data
Marcovitz, Hal.
  Teaching intelligent design / by Hal Marcovitz.
      p. cm. — (Essential viewpoints)
  Includes bibliographical references and index.
  ISBN 978-1-60453-537-2
  1. Intelligent design (Teleology) 2. Cosmogony. 3. Natural selection. 4. Evolution (Biology)—Religious aspects. 5. Evolution (Biology) 6. Darwin, Charles, 1809-1882—Criticism and interpretation. I. Title.

  BF651.M37 2009
  231.7'652—dc22

                              2008034919

TABLE OF CONTENTS

In 2004, the Dover Area School Board mandated that intelligent design be taught in ninth-grade science classrooms in Dover, Pennsylvania.

The Dover Case

The tiny community of Dover, Pennsylvania, hardly seems the type of place that would spark a national debate over science and religion. The community sits in a rural corner of the state near the Maryland border. For years, the only

Dover natives who made national news were Scott Strausburg, an Olympic gold medalist in white-water kayaking, and Jeff Koons, a nationally renowned sculptor.

But in October 2004, the Dover Area School Board announced a policy change that would stir controversy in the school district and the rest of the country. The board called into question the process of evolution as first described and published by Charles Darwin in 1859. The policy change mandated that students be made aware of alternative beliefs that the school directors felt could help explain the development of life on Earth. The school board's resolution was adopted by a 6–3 margin. It read, "Students will be made aware of gaps/problems in Darwin's theory and of other theories of evolution including, but not limited to, intelligent design."[1]

Intelligent design is a belief held by many creationists that suggests life on Earth is too complicated to have evolved from the simplest creatures. Therefore, the evolution of people and other forms of life was helped by another entity—an "intelligent designer." Intelligent design is one of several beliefs held by creationists who reject, in whole or in part, evolutionary science. The concept of evolution suggests that all living things on Earth evolved from a single ancestor. Instead, creationists largely embrace that God created life. Creationists believe life has come about according to a divine plan.

A month after issuing the mandate to teach intelligent design as well as evolution, the Dover Area School Board issued a statement further explaining its policy. The board noted that Darwin's theory was only a theory, and that "intelligent design is an explanation of the origin of life that differs from Darwin's view."[2]

Most biologists and other scientists

Of Pandas and People

When the Dover Area School Board issued its mandate to teach intelligent design to ninth-grade science students, the board suggested that students be given access to the textbook *Of Pandas and People: The Central Question of Biological Origins.*

The authors of the book argue that the science of natural selection is incomplete. They suggest intelligent design can help fill in the gaps. For example, natural selection is largely supported by the examination of fossils of extinct creatures. But many fossils showing the transition of a species over time have not yet been discovered. According to the authors,

Intelligent design means that various forms of life began abruptly through an intelligent agency, with their distinctive features already intact—fish with fins and scales, birds with feathers, beaks, and wings, etc. Some scientists have arrived at this view since fossil forms first appear in the rock record with their distinctive features intact, rather than gradually developing.[3]

The board did not mandate that teachers assign the book, but made the book available in the middle school library.

got upset at those words. They stated that evolution is a theory that has always held up to testing. While there may be gaps in the knowledge of how living things have evolved, natural selection has been tested and proven numerous times since Darwin first published his findings. Further, they insisted that no theory of creationism, including intelligent design, has ever passed the test of scientific scrutiny. These scientists were joined in their belief. Many parents, members of the faculty, and other members of the Dover community also opposed the school board's mandate. Steven Stough, the parent of a Dover student, said,

> *You can dress up intelligent design and make it look like science, but it doesn't pass muster. In science class, you don't say to students, "Is there gravity, or do you think we have rubber bands on our feet?"*[4]

Within weeks of the school board's order to teach intelligent design, 11 parents of Dover students filed a lawsuit. It stated that the mandate violated the separation of church and state provision of the U.S. Constitution.

The Heart of the Controversy

The First Amendment of the Constitution guarantees freedom of religion and the separation of church and state. U.S. citizens are free to worship as they please. Yet, the courts have consistently ruled that religious doctrine cannot be taught in public schools, which are funded by the government. The courts have ruled creationist theories are religious in nature. Teaching these theories in public schools violates separation of church and state.

However, supporters of intelligent design and similar beliefs argue that creationism offers an alternative viewpoint to evolutionary science. They believe students should be given contrasting sides of an issue so they may draw their own conclusions.

William Buckingham was the Dover school director who first proposed that intelligent design be taught alongside evolution. He said,

> *In looking at the biology book the teachers wanted, I noticed that it was laced with Darwinism. . . . It wasn't on every page of the book, but, like, every couple of chapters, there was Darwin, in your face again. And it was to the exclusion of any other theory.*[5]

CONSERVATIVE MOVEMENT

In issuing its new policy, the Dover Area School Board became the first to order the teaching of intelligent design. The theory had been given widespread exposure in the 1991 book *Darwin on Trial* by University of California-Berkeley law professor Phillip Johnson. Throughout the 1990s, religious conservatives in the United States gained political power. Christian leaders looked for ways to promote their faith commitments, which they believed were being attacked in a secular society. In 2000, religious conservatives wholeheartedly supported the presidential campaign of George W. Bush. Four years later, Bush suggested that "scientific critiques of any theory should be a normal part of the science curriculum."[6] By his statement, many conservatives concluded that the government was now supportive of teaching creationist beliefs. A month after Bush made those remarks, the Dover Area School Board issued its mandate.

Support from the President

In August 2005, President George W. Bush told news reporters that creationism has a place in public school science classrooms: "Both sides ought to be properly taught . . . so people can understand what the debate is about. Part of education is to expose people to different schools of thought. You're asking me whether or not people ought to be exposed to different ideas, and the answer is yes."[7]

Some Dover Area High School science teachers refused to teach intelligent design.

A trial commenced in the U.S. District Court in Harrisburg, Pennsylvania, in September 2005. Throughout the two-month trial, experts on evolution testified for the parents who initiated the lawsuit. These experts insisted that intelligent design had no ground in science. Attorneys for the school board offered their own witnesses. Some included scientists who suggested that creationism could help fill in the gaps in natural selection. Biochemistry professor Michael J. Behe, a witness for the school board, stated that "the appearance of design in aspects of biology is overwhelming. . . . A reasonable person might wonder if [Darwin's] theory was missing a large piece of the puzzle."[8]

No Resolution to the Debate

Before the judge had a chance to rule, the school directors who supported the mandate were replaced in a school board election. During the campaign, the challengers declared they would not allow intelligent design to be taught in classrooms. During the election campaign, family members took sides and neighbors argued with neighbors. Still, there was no questioning the outcome of the campaign. The voters of Dover elected eight new members to the school board, all opposed to teaching intelligent design in the schools.

U.S. District Judge John E. Jones III ruled that the school board's mandate violated the constitutional

Campaign Promise

One of the parents who ran for the Dover Area School Board in the 2005 election was Bryan Rehm. He taught science in Dover but found a job in another school district after the 2004 mandate to teach intelligent design. As a candidate for the Dover Area School Board, Rehm promised to cancel the mandate, saying he couldn't work in a district that mandated religious ideas in the classroom.

guarantee of separation of church and state. He
wrote,

> *Intelligent design is grounded in theology, not science.*
> *Accepting for the sake of argument its proponents' . . .*
> *argument that to introduce intelligent design to students will*
> *encourage critical thinking, it still has utterly no place in a*
> *science curriculum. Moreover, intelligent design's backers*
> *have sought to avoid the scientific scrutiny which we have*
> *now determined that it cannot withstand. . . . The goal of*
> *the intelligent design movement is not to encourage critical*
> *thought but to [foster] a revolution which would supplant*
> *evolutionary theory with intelligent design.*[9]

The debate between supporters of creationism
and evolution did not begin in Dover. The issue has
been the subject of heated dispute since Darwin first
published findings that were contrary to the word of
the Bible. And the debate between creationists and
evolutionists did not end in Dover. As Judge Jones
issued his decision, new challenges to Darwinism
were raised in Kansas, Florida, and other states.

In 2006, an opponent of teaching creationism protests outside a California high school that currently teaches a class on evolution alternatives.

Charles Darwin's theory of evolution by natural selection has sparked controversy for 150 years.

CHARLES DARWIN AND
NATURAL SELECTION

*I*n 1859, Charles Darwin published the principles of evolution by natural selection. Reaction was swift and critical. A large portion of the scientific community attacked his ideas about evolution. Many scientists argued that natural selection could not be proven. Several religious leaders attacked Darwin as well. They believed it foolish to suggest men and women evolved from lower creatures. Natural selection contradicted the story of Genesis. The Bible's story of creation had been taught in Christian churches and other houses of worship for generations. Charles Hodge was a noted American theologian of the era. Hodge believed evolution ". . . banishes God from the world, it enables them [evolutionists] to account for design without referring it to the purpose or agency of God."[1]

But Darwin also had his supporters. Years before Darwin took up the study of nature, other scientists laid the groundwork for evolutionary science. In 1800, French zoologist Jean-Baptiste Antoine de Monet, known as the Chevalier de Lamarck, theorized that species change over time. However, Lamarck stopped short of suggesting how that may happen. Some of Lamarck's theories were inaccurate. For example, he did not believe a species became extinct but instead changed (evolved) into another species. Nevertheless, Lamarck's theories suggested that something other than a creator had a hand in the evolution of species.

The idea of evolution was not new when Darwin published his findings. Natural selection "awes me," declared British novelist Charles Kingsley in a letter to Darwin. "If you be right I must give up much that I have believed."[2]

VOYAGE OF THE *BEAGLE*

Charles Darwin was born in 1809 to a wealthy British family. As a young man he attended medical school but dropped out to study for the clergy. While studying at Cambridge University, Darwin became interested in natural science. Shortly after his graduation in 1831, he joined a scientific expedition aboard the HMS *Beagle*.

During the five-year voyage, Darwin studied hundreds of species and fossils. At this time, many scientists endorsed what was known as catastrophic theory. The theory suggested that animal and plant life on Earth had repeatedly been created and destroyed in sudden catastrophes. The most recent of these was the Great Flood, which is described in the Old Testament of the Bible.

However, other eminent scientists of the era, particularly geologist Charles Lyell, questioned catastrophic theory. Lyell suggested that life on Earth existed uninterrupted by the Great Flood or other catastrophic events. Lyell insisted, "The present is the key to the past."[5] However, most scientists, including Lyell, believed that different species were separately created by the hand of God.

Darwin's observations throughout the *Beagle* voyage led him to believe that many species carried common traits. He found fossils of extinct creatures bearing similar traits to living animals. He also found evidence that some species had died out relatively recently. Yet, there had been no recent catastrophic event. In the Galápagos Islands near Ecuador, Darwin found that the physical traits of finches differed from island to island. He also found that tortoises differed from place to place. Eventually, he drew the conclusion that the species were evolving differently.

The *Beagle* returned to London in 1836. Darwin continued his research. He was influenced by a 1798 paper by British economist Thomas Malthus titled "An Essay on the Principle of Population." Malthus suggested that

The Test of Time

Charles Darwin formed his ideas about natural selection during the five-year voyage of the HMS *Beagle*, which ended in 1836. Darwin's basic theory of natural selection has stood the test of time—for more than 150 years.

The illustration shows the evolution of a primate into a human being.

the growth of the world's population could not be supported by the availability of food. Therefore, the population would continually be held in check by famine, disease, war, and other social forces. This was an early version of the Darwinian concept that eventually became known as "survival of the fittest."

Darwin published *On the Origin of the Species* in 1859. In the book, he contended that living things evolve through natural selection. He applied Malthus's arguments to the natural world, suggesting that species must constantly struggle to find food. Species that survive this constant struggle pass on to the next generation the traits that enabled them to prosper. These advantages are very subtle and take many years to develop. Over a period of time, the key traits surface and allow the species to adapt and evolve. The species that do not adapt die out.

Finally, Darwin suggested that all living things on Earth—plants and animals—evolved from a single, common ancestor. Darwin wrote,

> It is obvious that the several species . . . though inhabiting the most distant quarters of the world, must originally have proceeded from the same source, as they have descended from the same progenitor.[6]

CONFIRMING DARWIN'S CONCLUSIONS

In the 150 years since Darwin published his findings, scientists have tested and retested the principles of natural selection. The numerous

Publishing *Origin*

Charles Darwin was well aware of the shocking nature of natural selection. It was one reason why he delayed publication of *On the Origin of the Species* for 20 years. However, when Darwin learned that another naturalist, Alfred Russel Wallace, was preparing a manuscript that drew similar conclusions, he brought his book to the printer.

experiments have repeatedly confirmed Darwin's conclusions. Studies of fossils turned up transitional species. These are animals that lived millions of years ago that shared traits found in both land and water creatures.

Other transitional species have linked apes with humans. In 1974, the skeleton of a human ancestor was discovered in Ethiopia. Based on an examination of the pelvis, the discoverers concluded that the specimen was female. It was nicknamed

Darwin's Bulldog

Two years after *On the Origin of the Species* was published, the book gained a measure of credibility thanks to English biologist Thomas Huxley. He made a strong case for natural selection during a debate before the British Association for the Advancement of Science. During the so-called "Oxford debate," Huxley's firm defense of natural selection earned him the nickname "Darwin's bulldog."

Huxley debated Samuel Wilberforce, the Anglican bishop of Oxford. Wilberforce attacked Darwinism for two hours. Apparently sensing that he had put his audience to sleep, the bishop decided to end his speech with a joke. He asked Huxley whether he had been descended from apes on his grandmother's side or grandfather's side. Huxley responded,

> I should feel it no shame to have sprung from such an origin but I should feel it a shame to have sprung from one who prostituted the gifts of culture and eloquence to the service of prejudice and falsehood.[3]

Huxley later said he intended his comments to be taken with humor, but witnesses saw that the biologist was angry. Darwin, however, clearly appreciated Huxley's spirit. "I honor your pluck," he told Huxley. "I would as soon have died as tried to answer the bishop in such an assembly."[4]

"Lucy" and considered to be more than 3 million years old. Judging by the bones in Lucy's head and neck, she was more closely related to chimpanzees than humans. But judging by her knees, she appeared to walk upright, not on all fours. This means she had human characteristics as well. Brown University biologist Kevin Miller stated,

> *The notion that all these lines of evidence could converge and give a common answer to the question of where we came from is truly powerful. That is the reason why scientific support for . . . evolution is so overwhelming.*[7]

Many genetic studies have found that living things share common deoxyribonucleic acid (DNA) and other similarities. In 2008, Harvard Medical School and Beth Israel Deaconess Medical Center scientists compared the protein they extracted from a fossilized *Tyrannosaurus rex*

The Descent of Man

The suggestion that humans and apes share a common ancestor was barely touched on in *On the Origin of the Species*. Darwin knew it was one of his most shocking findings and worried that the public would reject it. In 1871, Darwin published another book, *The Descent of Man*, in which he wrote at length about human ancestors.

bone with the protein drawn from chicken and ostrich bones. The proteins were found to be very similar. This added weight to the idea that birds descended from dinosaurs. "We had made a very loose connection at first," said Harvard scientist John Asara. "Now we're able to make out robust evolutionary relationships with very high confidence, basically grouping the T. rex dinosaur with birds."[8]

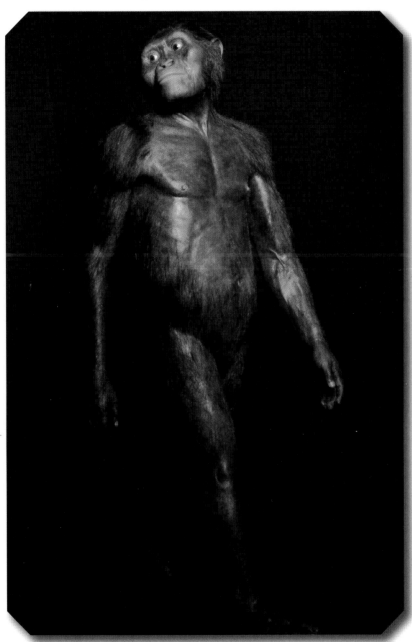

*A model of Lucy, a 3-million-year-old transitional species
that links humans and apes*

Creation of Adam, *one of the paintings on the ceiling of the Sistine Chapel, portrays a humanlike God creating the first human.*

CREATIONIST BELIEFS

While creationists are not always Christians, organized Christian groups have been the most visible in the public debate. It is the conflict between evolutionary theory and the Bible that is at the center of their concern.

The Bible is said to be written by humans who were divinely inspired. At various points, some faiths determined that the Bible is without error. One of these is the largest Protestant denomination in the United States, the Baptist Church. This denomination believes not one word in the Bible is incorrect or false. The church believes the Bible can be read literally.

Many creationists are driven by a literal reading of the Bible. Because one's faith in Christianity's doctrine depends upon belief in the Bible, there is motivation to fight anything that seems to contradict it. The Bible must be authentic in every detail. If one part of the Bible is incorrect, every other part could be called into question as well.

People Are a Special Part of Creation

The story of Genesis is the first book in the Old Testament of the Bible. This book is holy scripture in Jewish and Christian traditions. In Genesis, it is written that God made all of creation in six days:

And God made the beast of the earth after his kind, and cattle after their kind, and every thing that creepeth upon the earth after his kind: and God saw that it was good. And God said,

Let us make man in our image, after our likeness: and let them have dominion over the fish of the sea, and over the fowl of the air, and over the cattle, and over all the earth, and over every creeping thing that creepeth upon the earth. So God created man in his own image, in the image of God created he him; male and female created he them.[1]

An important part of the creation story in the Bible is the special status of human beings among other creatures. God created humans separately and "in his own image." In this way, humans have a special likeness to and relationship with God.

Evolution places humans among other species. For those who believe humans have a special relationship with God, it is upsetting to be told they are a product of impersonal mechanisms, like every other organism. Many creationists believe that evolutionary theory eliminates meaning from life.

Types of Creationists

People who believe humans and other species were created as described in the scriptures believe in what is known as young earth creationism. This belief holds that Earth is between 6,000 and 10,000 years old. The dating of Earth is based on merging a timeline of biblical events into a real-time calendar of world history.

Scientific evidence suggests that Earth is more than 4 billion years old. Yet, the idea of young earth creationism, in which Earth may be less than 10,000 years old, has many supporters. The 15-million-member Seventh-day Adventist Church believes in a literal interpretation of the Bible. A church statement says,

> The Seventh-day Adventist Church affirms a divine

How Other Religions Address Evolution

The book of Genesis tells the Jewish and Christian interpretation of the creation of life on Earth. Other religions subscribe to different beliefs about the origin of life. Hindus believe life in the universe has been eternal, but occasionally interrupted and recreated. Similar to Genesis, the Islamic holy book known as the Quran states that the universe was created in six days. Yet, Muslims believe the Old Testament is flawed. A variety of beliefs exist among Muslims, ranging from an acceptance of scientific evidence to belief in creationist concepts.

Buddhism emphasizes the constant change in life. This belief may align with the change concept of evolution. The 4-million member Jainism faith of India does not believe in a creator. Members suggest the universe has always existed.

Clearly, the Jewish and Christian notion of creation is just one interpretation of how life began. Eugenie C. Scott is the executive director of the National Center for Science Education and an authority on creationist beliefs. Scott stated,

> All people try to make sense of the world around them, and that includes speculating about the course of events that brought the world and its inhabitants to their present state.[2]

creation as described in the biblical narrative of Genesis 1.
God is Creator of all things, and has revealed in Scripture the
authentic account of His creative activity. In six days the Lord
made "the heaven and the earth" and all living things upon
the earth. . . . [3]

BROAD INTERPRETATION OF THE BIBLE

While evolutionists accept the general framework
of natural selection, they consider many theories
about the specifics of evolution. Likewise, while
creationists believe species were generated according
to a divine plan, they hold several ideas regarding
specifics. In addition to young earth creationism,
other creationist beliefs include old earth
creationism, flood geology, creation science, theistic
evolution, and intelligent design.

Old earth creationism accepts the scientific age
of Earth but holds that life was created relatively
recently. A variation on the theory provides a broad
interpretation on the Bible's explanation that the
world was created in six days. It suggests that the six-
day span could have taken billions of years.

Flood geology is a belief held mostly by young
earth creationists. It suggests that mountains, valleys,

An exhibit at the Creation Museum in Kentucky shows two paleontologists reaching different conclusions from the same fossil.

and continents formed after the waters of the Great Flood receded. Ronald L. Numbers, a historian and authority on creationist beliefs, states,

> For those who wanted to take the Bible literally, flood geology meant having to make no assumptions. . . . If you accepted flood geology, you could take the Genesis story—as well as the story of Noah and the universal flood that destroyed most of life on earth—literally. [4]

Creation science is a relatively new movement in the creationist community. It attempts to prove creationist beliefs using scientific means. Creation science grew out of a series of U.S. court cases in which judges ruled that schools must teach evolution based on scientific principles. In response, creationists started seeking scientific evidence to support their beliefs. Creation science theories rely mostly on evidence creationists believe is missing in fossils. The movement suggests that the absence of transitional fossils proves species evolved separately from one another. Evolutionists counter that transitional fossils, such as Lucy, do exist.

Proponents of theistic evolution accept the scientific evidence of natural selection. However, they believe evolution is still guided by a divine plan. Some very influential Western religions, including the Roman Catholic Church, have accepted scientific explanations for the creation of the universe. Yet they still believe God guides life on Earth. Many Jewish theological leaders also accept the scientific explanation for evolution. They counsel Jews to look to God for spiritual guidance.

Intelligent Design

The basic principle of intelligent design is that life is too complicated to have evolved without assistance. The world is well organized, beautiful, and complex. For creationists, claiming the artful coordination of nature is the result of a series of genetic accidents takes out the genius of creation. The genius of creation is God. Creationists think it is absurd that evolutionary theorists believe the world was created without a creator.

In the early 1800s, British theologian William Paley gave the analogy of a watch and a watchmaker. Suppose someone walking in the countryside finds a watch on the side of the road. The person picks up and examines the watch to find it intricate and sophisticated. Because of this, the person would assume there was a watchmaker who designed and created it. Examining life on Earth would bring a similar conclusion. According to creationists, life on Earth was designed and created by a maker.

Phillip Johnson was the first person to introduce intelligent design to a widespread audience. He pointed out that when Darwin conceived natural

Creation Science Is Not Science

Ronald L. Numbers, author of *The Creationists: The Evolution of Scientific Creationism*, says creation science should not be regarded as real science. While there was a time when religion and science could be mixed, there is no reason for it to happen today, believes Numbers.

selection more than 150 years ago, biologists believed life was simpler than it has turned out to be. Darwin had little understanding of the complexities of cells and DNA. If Darwin had, he may have realized natural selection does not offer all the answers. Johnson stated,

> *Thanks to the work of biochemists and molecular biologists since that time, we know that the cell is so enormously complex that it makes a spaceship or a supercomputer look rather low-tech in comparison. So I think the cell is perhaps the biggest hurdle of all for the Darwinists to get over. How do you get the first cell?[5]*

Intelligent Design Is Science

Phillip Johnson's 1991 book, *Darwin on Trial*, introduced the concept of intelligent design to a widespread audience. Johnson insists that intelligent design is a science. He says, "If evolution by natural selection is a scientific doctrine, then the critique of that doctrine, and even of the fundamental assumption on which it's based, is a legitimate part of science as well."[6]

In the 1800s, theologian William Paley compared the concept of God and life on Earth to a watchmaker and a watch.

A science class learns about creationism and evolution in 1948.

EVOLUTION OF THE DEBATE

By the early years of the twentieth century, fundamentalist church leaders as well as many political leaders rejected Darwinism. They called on their followers to adopt a literal interpretation of the story of Genesis. In the United

States, opposition to Darwinism was particularly strong. The Reverend Billy Sunday and other preachers delivered fiery sermons denouncing Darwinism and ridiculing scientists who endorsed natural selection. "That sort of philosopher is a *foolosopher*," Sunday insisted during a sermon in 1917.[1]

Another opponent of Darwinism was former presidential candidate William Jennings Bryan. He urged state legislatures to adopt laws opposing Darwinism. Several states enacted such laws. In 1925, Tennessee adopted the Butler Act, which prohibited the teaching of natural selection in the state's public schools. The act stated,

William Jennings Bryan

William Jennings Bryan was one of the most well-known political figures and orators of the early twentieth century. He served as secretary of state under President Woodrow Wilson. Bryan unsuccessfully sought the presidency three times. His opposition to natural selection was sparked mostly out of an abhorrence of the Darwinian principle of "survival of the fittest."

> *It shall be unlawful for any teacher in any of the universities . . . and all other public schools of the state . . . to teach any theory that denies the story of the Divine Creation of man as taught in the Bible, and to teach instead that man has descended from a lower order of animal.*[2]

The newly formed American Civil Liberties Union (ACLU) called for a teacher to challenge the law. In the town of Dayton, Tennessee, science teacher John T. Scopes volunteered. Scopes was then charged with violating the Butler Act, although he was never quite sure that the subject of natural selection actually came up in class.

Nevertheless, Scopes was prosecuted. The state hired William Jennings Bryan as the prosecutor. To defend Scopes, the ACLU retained Clarence Darrow, the preeminent defense attorney of the day.

The Scopes Monkey Trial, as it became known, made national headlines but ultimately failed to solve the issue. The judge refused to allow Darrow to put Darwinism on trial. The case was confined to whether Scopes violated the Butler Act by teaching natural selection. Darrow was successful, though, in persuading Bryan to take the witness stand as a self-proclaimed expert on the Bible. During his testimony, Bryan often sounded foolish as he failed to provide evidence supporting

Clarence Darrow

Eminent defense attorney Clarence Darrow lost the Scopes case in the Dayton courtroom but won on a technicality before the Tennessee Supreme Court. The court tossed out the conviction without making a judgment on the key issue in the case—whether natural selection is true science. Still, Darrow felt confident that the Scopes decision marked the beginning of the end for teaching creationism in public schools.

Science teacher John T. Scopes challenged the Butler Act by teaching evolution in his classroom.

the literal interpretation of Genesis. "There is no place for the miracle in this train of evolution," Bryan declared, "and the Old Testament and New are filled with miracles."[3]

ATTITUDES CHANGE

Scopes was convicted and made to pay a $100 fine for violating the Butler Act. Backed by the

ACLU, Darrow appealed the conviction, hoping to find a court that would establish Darwinism as a truth. The case was argued before the Tennessee Supreme Court, which overturned the Dayton, Tennessee, judge on a technicality. The Supreme Court stated that the jury, and not the judge, should have set the penalty. Although the conviction was overturned, the ACLU did not welcome the Tennessee Supreme Court's decision. By overturning the case on a technicality, the state Supreme

Inherit the Wind

The Scopes Monkey Trial has become a familiar chapter in U.S. popular culture. It was adapted into a successful Broadway play and a film titled *Inherit the Wind*. The 1955 play written by Jerome Lawrence and Robert E. Lee draws its title from the biblical plea for tolerance found in Proverbs. "He that troubleth his own house shall inherit the wind: and the fool shall be servant to the wise of heart." (11:29 AV).

Although Lawrence and Lee changed the names of the main characters, the playwrights drew dialogue for the script from the Scopes trial transcript. However, there is no question that the play is a fictional treatment of the trial. In the play, the townspeople denounce the character of the teacher. Actually, John T. Scopes was encouraged to break the Butler Act by business leaders and other citizens of Dayton, Tennessee. They believed a sensational, headline-grabbing trial would draw national attention to their town and be good for business.

Also, Scopes was never actually "arrested." When he agreed to be prosecuted for breaking the Butler Act, he was playing tennis. He also never spent a day in jail. In the play and film, though, the Scopes character is held in jail throughout the trial.

Court evaded the principle issue of whether natural selection is a legitimate science. And, with no conviction to appeal, the ACLU could not take the case to the U.S. Supreme Court. The Butler Act remained on the books in Tennessee for nearly another half-century.

Other states kept their antievolution statutes as well. By 1930, just five years after the Scopes decision, approximately 70 percent of science classrooms in the United States omitted the teaching of evolution.

During the next few decades, antievolutionary thinking dominated classrooms. But in 1957, U.S. attitudes started changing. This was due, in large part, to the launch of Sputnik, the first satellite. Launched by the Soviet Union, Sputnik demonstrated that the United States had fallen behind the Soviet Union in scientific research. Congress responded by establishing a number of programs to enhance science education. Science textbooks were reviewed and found to be of poor quality. Most biology textbooks avoided any mention of evolution. By 1963, new biology textbooks had been introduced into classrooms. The new books discussed Darwinism. Meanwhile, most of the state laws banning the teaching of evolution had been repealed.

There was a new emphasis on science education. Still, some religious and political leaders were not yet willing to accept this. By the 1960s, four states still maintained laws against teaching Darwinism: Tennessee, Louisiana, Mississippi, and Arkansas.

In 1965, Arkansas teacher Susan Epperson challenged her state's law. Epperson argued that it violated her First Amendment right to freedom of speech. In 1968, the U.S. Supreme Court heard the case of *Epperson v. Arkansas*. The court handed down the first ruling, declaring the teaching of evolution a First Amendment issue. When Arkansas banned the teaching of a scientifically proven concept because religious leaders found it objectionable, it violated the separation of church and state mandate of the U.S. Constitution. The court found:

> *Government in our democracy must be neutral in matters of religious theory, doctrine and practice. It may not be hostile to any religion or the advocacy of non-religion, and it may not aid, foster, or promote one religion or religious theory against another or even against the militant opposite.*[4]

Antievolution books are sold at a booth outside the courtroom of the Scopes trial in Tennessee.

Ejecting Creationism

Epperson v. Arkansas was the first in a series of court decisions that would eliminate creationism from public school classrooms. Following the Epperson decision, advocates of creationism proposed "equal time" laws. These would mandate the teaching of creationism alongside natural selection. In 1981, Arkansas adopted an equal time law. It was immediately challenged in court and soon declared unconstitutional because it violated the separation

**Creationism Has
Its Place**

Most opponents to teaching creationism believe there is a place for discussing creationist viewpoints in public schools, just not in biology class. They find it acceptable to provide students with information about creationist doctrine and the debate over evolution in classes devoted to the study of religion, political science, or similar subjects.

of church and state. Louisiana's 1982 equal time law was also challenged. That case was appealed to the U.S. Supreme Court, which also tossed out the law.

With the courts ruling that all discussion of evolution in classrooms be based on scientific principles, creationists changed their strategy. They contended that scientific evidence does support the creationist view. This strategy led to the development of creation science, intelligent design, and similar theories. But the 2005 Dover decision found no scientific basis for such beliefs.

*A model of the first satellite, Sputnik, that was launched
by the Soviet Union in 1957*

The Galápagos Islands are where Darwin first observed what he eventually called natural selection.

An Imperfect Science

ven the most dedicated scientists admit that evolution is an imperfect science. After all, there were no scientists living millions of years ago to record when human ancestors developed opposable thumbs. There were no scientists to record when a creature first slithered out of the ocean and developed feet in place of fins. And there were no scientists recording the event when a human ancestor decided to walk on two feet instead of four. Acclaimed author and biologist Richard Dawkins states,

> It's often said that because evolution happened in the past, and we didn't see it happen, there is no direct evidence for it. That, of course, is nonsense. It's rather like a detective coming on the scene of a crime, obviously after the crime has been committed, and working out what must have happened by looking at the clues that remain. In the story of evolution, the clues are a billionfold.[1]

Yet, evolutionary science is a far different science than, for example, physics. In 1687, Isaac Newton first described the physical laws of motion. One includes that for every action there is an equal and opposite reaction. These laws have held up under centuries of study. Even the most devoted creationists can see Newton's law in practice when a baseball comes into contact with a bat.

FILLING IN THE GAPS

Creation science suggests that fossils of extinct species include too many gaps. Creationists contend that, when it comes to natural selection, the evidence can be questioned. There are significant gaps in parts of evolutionary science, so there is room for other interpretations, creationists say. The late Henry Morris, founder of the Texas-based Institute for Creation Research, said, "The fossil record has traditionally been considered the best evidence for evolution, but the utter absence of true transitional forms continues to be an embarrassment."[2]

What Is a Theory?

Evolution supporters insist that natural selection is not a theory but proven science. Creationists counter that natural selection is one of many theories that explains how humans and other living things arrived on Earth.

The National Academy of Sciences draws a distinction between fact and theory. A fact is "an observation that has been repeatedly confirmed and for all practical purposes is accepted as true."[3] Biologists insist that natural selection has been tested many times and has always been confirmed as true.

A theory is a "well-substantiated explanation of some aspect of the natural world that can incorporate facts, laws, inferences, and tested hypotheses."[4] Therefore, the National Academy says, simply referring to a principle as a theory does not necessarily mean it has failed the test of science.

For example, one part of Albert Einstein's theory of special relativity states that no object can travel at the speed of light. Special relativity has been accepted in physics as a fact. It has been tested and proven many times, mostly by mathematical calculations. However, it is impossible to prove Einstein's theory in the real world. The technology does not exist to power a spacecraft at the speed of light—about 670 million miles (1.078 billion km) per hour—to determine if the craft can obtain light speed.

The National Academy of Sciences counters this belief. It states,

> Creationists sometimes cite what they claim to be an incomplete fossil record as evidence living things were created in their modern forms. But this argument ignores the rich and extremely detailed record of evolutionary history that paleontologists and other biologists have constructed over the past two centuries and are continuing to construct. Paleontological research has filled in many of the parts of the fossil record that were incomplete in Charles Darwin's time. [5]

Return to Galápagos

Evolutionists believe in the general framework for natural selection of the evolutionary model that Darwin laid out 150 years ago. But there is no question that over the years scientists have developed a range of theories on how life evolved within that framework. By the 1940s,

Fossils Offer No Proof

Henry Morris, founder of the Institute for Creation Research, insisted that fossils offer no proof of evolution. He contended that science requires observation. Since scientists could not observe the living creatures that made the fossils, Morris believed the fossils themselves could give no proof of scientific theories, such as evolution.

the modern synthetic theory of evolution gained
favor among most scientists. Also known as neo-
Darwinism, the synthetic theory holds that evolution
is ongoing and occurs slowly. Following the theory,
a species would pull together many complex parts to
synthesize, or come together, over time.

In 1972, paleontologists Stephen Jay Gould and
Niles Eldredge had advanced a competing theory
of punctuated equilibrium. This notion suggests
that there are long periods of evolutionary stability
interrupted by sudden periods of rapid change in
the species. Work by other scientists has supported
this theory. On the Galápagos Islands, where Darwin
made some of his most significant observations,
Princeton University biologists Peter and Rosemary
Grant observed changes in the evolution of birds.
They noticed that the beaks of finches evolved
over a period of just a few years. Author Jonathan
Weiner chronicled the Grants' work in his Pulitzer
Prize-winning book, *The Beak of the Finch*. The book
points out an instance when the islands were hit by
a drought that wiped out most finches. A few birds
survived and produced offspring. In these birds,
the Grants noticed the beaks had evolved. They had
grown larger and deeper, enabling them to crack

Peter and Rosemary Grant observed the evolution of finches' beaks on the Galápagos Islands.

open the tough seeds that survived the drought.
Weiner wrote,

> *No one had ever seen Darwin's process work that fast. And*
> *this was not evolution in a test tube, or in a lab cage full of*

fruit flies, or in the moths of a polluted city. The Grants were watching natural selection in nature, in an environment as pristine as you can find on planet Earth.[6]

LEFT BEHIND BY THE FLOOD

Other branches of science also have their share of competing theories. In astronomy and theoretical physics, disagreement over the origins of the universe has been going on for years. Many astronomers support the big bang theory, which states that the universe was created in a single cataclysmic event. But many astronomers have sought to modify the theory over the years. And even those who are in agreement with the big bang theory are often at a loss to explain what came before the big bang. Many theoretical physicists have advanced ideas. However, their theories have

Evolution Is Being Witnessed

Jonathan Weiner is the Pulitzer Prize-winning author of *The Beak of the Finch*. He believes evolution can be seen in places like the Galápagos Islands, where scientists have recorded evolutionary changes in birds from generation to generation. He says, "Today, evolutionists are watching the evolution of guppies, grass, flies, moths, mice and elephants; of slime molds and soapberry bugs; of the cosmopolitan bacteria that lives in the human gut, and of the human beings too. Taken together, these new studies suggest Darwin did not know the strength of his own theory. He vastly underestimated the power of natural selection. Its action is neither rare nor slow. It leads to evolution daily and hourly, all around us, and we can watch."[7]

often been based on mathematical computations because there is little physical evidence to support their notions.

Creationists point out that scientists differ on how the universe was formed or how evolution works. If they cannot agree on this, creationists claim, they are in no position to dismiss creationism as an alternative that lacks legitimacy. Morris stated, "Evolutionists ardently defend their house against outsiders, but squabble vigorously with each other inside the house."[8]

Creationists have been willing to step in and fill in the gaps of evolutionary science. With their ideas, creationists believe they can reconcile the differences held by competing schools of thought. For example, many creationists insist that the fossils that have been found by scientists emerged after the Great Flood.

Morris pointed out that fossils of extinct creatures are usually found in rocks where one would expect to find them. Simple marine creatures are found in the deepest layers of rock because they lived at the lowest elevations in the depths of the sea. Fossils of birds and mammals are found in higher layers of rock. These creatures lived on the surface of the planet. Clearly, Morris said, the fossils always turn up where they are found in nature because these species perished suddenly during a cataclysmic event—the Great Flood. Morris contended,

> How much more simple and direct it would be to explain the fossil-bearing rocks as the record in stone of the destruction of the . . . world by the Great Flood. The various fossil assemblages represent, not evolutionary stages developing over many ages, but rather ecological habitats in various parts of the world in one age.[9]

Supporters of evolutionary science claim these theories are similar to myths. They counter that while there may be competing theories regarding evolution, the overall science is sound and supported by evidence. John Rennie, editor-in-chief of *Scientific American*, states,

> Evolutionary biologists passionately debate diverse topics: how speciation happens, the rates of evolutionary change, the ancestral relationships of birds and dinosaurs, whether Neanderthals were a species apart from modern humans, and much more. These disputes are like those found in all other branches of science. Acceptance of evolution as a factual occurrence and a guiding principle is nonetheless universal in biology.[10]

Fossils found in different layers of rocks help supporters make an argument for creationism.

Herbert Spencer first coined the term "survival of the fittest."

SOCIAL DARWINISM

While the evolution-creationism debate resides primarily in schools, it does reach beyond the classroom and into social principles, such as survival of the fittest and social Darwinism.

The phrase "survival of the fittest" does not appear in Darwin's *On the Origin of the Species*. However, the phrase was first used in 1864, five years after Darwin published his research. Philosopher Herbert Spencer coined the term in his book, *Principles of Biology*. It was Spencer's intention to apply the principles of natural selection to politics, the economy, and other social conditions. The concept later became known as social Darwinism.

In social Darwinism, the strongest countries survive wars, the savviest and wealthiest businessmen make the most money, and the smartest minds rise to the top in professions. Initially, leaders on many sides of the political and social spectrums embraced social Darwinism. Millionaires such as Andrew Carnegie and John D. Rockefeller felt it adequately explained the reasons for their success. Socialist author Karl Marx said it provided him with evidence to suggest kings had no inherited or divine right to rule. Social Darwinism suggested that

The United States' Leading Social Darwinist

After Herbert Spencer published his theories, Yale University Professor William Graham Sumner emerged as the chief advocate for social Darwinism in the United States. Sumner said, "Let it be understood that we cannot go outside of this alternative: liberty, inequality, survival of the fittest; not liberty, equality, survival of the unfittest. The former carries society forward and favors all its best members; the latter carries society downwards and favors all its worst members."[1]

those most qualified to lead should govern countries. Marx read *On the Origin of the Species* in 1860. He wrote, "Darwin's book is very important and serves me as a basis in natural science for the struggle in history."[2]

To many U.S. citizens, social Darwinism presents something of a moral dilemma. The United States was founded on the principles that all men and women are created equal and that anyone can go as far as their talents and hard work can take them. Those principles guided the Founding Fathers. They knew that only those born to great wealth and noble families largely controlled European society.

Creationists do not like thinking of the world as a place that works alone according to adaptation fueled by fierce competition. They often relate this view to those that believe in evolutionary theory. Many creationists find this a hostile environment because survival is the end goal instead of flourishing or salvation.

Matters Outside of Science

An Englishman born in 1820, Spencer was a teacher and editor who embraced the theories of Lamarck, Lyell, and Darwin. He took their work a step further, applying evolutionary principles to

Standard Oil founder John D. Rockefeller was a proponent
of social Darwinism.

matters outside of science. Darwin had suggested
that species which failed to adapt faced extinction.
Similarly, Spencer believed that individuals, groups,
and societies that did not adapt to changing social
situations would also become extinct. "The whole

effort of nature is to get rid of [the unfit], to clear the world of them and to make room for better," wrote Spencer. "It is best that they should die."[3] According to Spencer, the weak, ill, and otherwise unfit members of society would eventually die out. A society of intelligent and successful high achievers would remain.

Spencer's theories were controversial. Critics suggested that humans are different from apes, birds, and other living things because they possess intelligence and moral codes the others do not. Thomas Huxley, the ardent defender of natural selection in the Oxford debate, found Spencer's ideas abhorrent. Huxley insisted, "The conscience of man revolts against the moral indifference of nature."[4]

Social Darwinism Today

Many religious leaders also denounced social Darwinism. In 1891, Pope Leo XIII issued an encyclical, a letter explaining Catholic doctrine. He called on industrial leaders to treat workers fairly and morally. Still, by the early years of the twentieth century, industrial giants felt Spencer's theories justified their business approach to win at all costs. As for the workers, the growth of the U.S. labor movement during the twentieth century shows that social Darwinism was not limited to wealthy industrialists. Workers banded together and formed labor unions. They became powerful enough to compete with management, head to head, at the bargaining table.

Social Darwinism exists today. If a large retailer moves into a community, small and locally owned stores may find they can no longer compete and are often driven out of business. In professional sports, the teams with the strongest and most skilled athletes and expert coaches usually win the championships. The New York Yankees can afford

"On Capital and Labor"

In his 1891 encyclical "On Capital and Labor," Pope Leo XIII argued against the principles of social Darwinism. He insisted that the government has the responsibility to protect workers, the poor, and others who may be abused by industrial leaders. The encyclical stated,

When there is [a] question of defending the rights of individuals, the poor and badly off have a claim to especial consideration. The richer class have many ways of shielding themselves, and stand less in need of help from the State; whereas the mass of the poor have no resources of their own to fall back upon, and must chiefly depend upon the assistance of the State. And it is for this reason that wage-earners, since they mostly belong in the mass of the needy, should be specially cared for and protected by the government.[5]

Social Darwinism exists today when small retail stores like Fireside's Hardware compete against large national chains like Home Depot.

to spend tens of millions of dollars each year on high-priced and talented ballplayers. Other teams from smaller cities have far fewer resources and usually find themselves struggling to compete.

Not everyone agrees with the concept of survival of the fittest in society. Religious leaders argue that the concept may lead others away from an ethical and moral foundation. Yet, if creationism is taught to young people, they may find themselves provided with ethical guidance that will give them an appreciation for charity, fair play, peace, and love of others. Religious leaders hold that there are many ethical lessons to be learned in the story of creation. In the book of Genesis, God picks Noah to survive the Great Flood because he regards him as righteous:

> *And God saw that the wickedness of man was great in the earth, and that every imagination of the thoughts of his heart was only evil continually. And it repented the Lord that he had made man on the earth, and it grieved him at his heart. And the Lord said, I will destroy man whom I have created from the face of the earth; both man, and beast, and the creeping thing, and the fowls of the air; for it repenteth me that I have made them.*[6]

But Noah found favor in the eyes of the Lord. William L. Johnson, associate dean of academic affairs at Ambassador University, a Christian college in Texas, states,

> *Competition, natural selection, and survival of the fittest are not presented as diverse observations among others, but as universal laws. Instead of competing with each other and distancing ourselves from one another, might we promote a sense of community and distance ourselves from the form of*

competition that embraces fear, manipulation, exploitation, segregation and intimidation?

The triumph of evolutionary ideas meant the end of the traditional belief in the world as a purposeful created order, and God's will was replaced by the capriciousness of a roulette wheel. The acceptance of this great claim and the consequent elimination of God from nature has played a decisive role in the secularization of modern society. Darwinian theory broke man's link with God and set him adrift in a cosmos without purpose or end.[7]

Many creationist supporters think intelligent design in schools may reduce the number of students who believe social Darwinism principles. Even more important, creationists believe it may stop social Darwinism taken to the negative extreme. ⌐

Some Christian leaders believe creationism in schools will teach students morals.

An exhibit shows a package of the sedative Luminal,
which Nazi doctors used to kill the disabled.

EUGENICS, STEM CELL
RESEARCH, AND CLONING

*T*aking the concept of social Darwinism a step
further were the proponents of eugenics.
This idea proposed that imperfect humans should
be weeded out of society. The idea was first proposed

by Francis Galton, a cousin of Charles Darwin. Galton published his theories in an 1869 book titled *Hereditary Genius*. He suggested that society give "the more suitable races or strains of blood a better chance of prevailing speedily over the less suitable."[1]

Galton proposed that the fittest not only survive, but they make sure the unfit do not. If this theory was advanced today, the notion would seem barbaric. But when Galton first proposed eugenics, the idea found favor among many influential people. Authors H. G. Wells and George Bernard Shaw, cereal businessman William Keith Kellogg, and Planned Parenthood founder Margaret Sanger supported eugenics.

Galton devised the term from the Greek word *eu*, which means "good" and the suffix *genes*, which are the hereditary components that provide all living things with their characteristics. He believed eugenics to be the logical next step following natural selection. Darwin proved that over time—in some cases, millions of years—various species improved because they evolved using the best traits provided by their ancestors. In Galton's view, humans could give natural selection a little nudge. He believed if mentally retarded persons were not allowed to

The American Eugenics Society

In 1921, supporters of eugenics established the American Eugenics Society. The organization aimed to promote the theories of Francis Galton.

One of the society's programs was the Fitter Families contest. To enter, families had to fill out forms to prove their physical and mental health. They also had to show that their ancestors were similarly healthy people. To promote the contests, Fitter Families judges attended state and county agricultural fairs, where they gave awards to the winners. The Eugenics Society also sponsored essay contests for students and gave awards to members of the clergy for preaching about the attributes of eugenics.

And in 1972 the Eugenics Society changed its name to the Society for the Study of Social Biology. The society no longer promotes eugenics or holds contests to find the fittest families. Rather, it encourages dialogue on ethical issues that stem from genetic research.

marry and have children, eventually there would be no mentally retarded people. At least, there would be none whose mental faculties failed to develop because of their parents' DNA. The end result, Galton insisted, would be improvement of the human race. Galton wrote,

> That is precisely the aim of Eugenics. Its first object is to check the birth-rate of the Unfit, instead of allowing them to come into being, though doomed in large numbers to perish prematurely. The second object is the improvement of the race by furthering the productivity of the Fit by early marriages and healthful rearing of their children. Natural Selection rests upon excessive production and wholesale destruction; Eugenics on bringing no more individuals into the world than can be properly cared for, and those only of the best stock. [2]

CREATING DANGEROUS PRACTICES

By the 1920s, at least 30 states had adopted laws sanctioning the sterilization of mentally retarded persons and other debilitated individuals. The idea behind the laws was to save society the burden of supporting their offspring. Many states also barred the marriages of mentally retarded persons. Some of these laws remained on the books until the 1970s.

Meanwhile, eugenics was also at the root of other unfair laws and governmental

The Carrie Buck Case

Carrie Buck was a Virginia woman who was judged "feebleminded." A Virginia eugenics law mandated the sterilization of severely mentally disabled people. Buck had given birth out of wedlock. Her daughter was judged to be mentally impaired. Buck's mother was believed to be mentally disabled. Under law, Buck was ordered to undergo sterilization.

She sued the state. In 1927, the U.S. Supreme Court voted 8–1 to uphold the state's eugenics law. Chief Justice Oliver Wendell Holmes wrote, "It is better for all the world . . . [if] society can prevent those who are manifestly unfit from continuing their kind. . . . Three generations of imbeciles are enough."[3]

As a result of the ruling, Buck was sterilized. Later, it was revealed that Buck had gotten pregnant as the result of a rape not because of a lack of mental acuity. Also, school officials determined that Buck's daughter Vivian was a bright child. In later years, mental health experts who interviewed Buck concluded that she was not mentally retarded. "The case was a sham constructed to play on fears that America was being swamped and burdened by poor, incompetent people," said Paul Lombardo, a University of Virginia historian.[4] He had interviewed Buck shortly before her death. Virginia's eugenics law was repealed in 1974 after years of not being enforced.

actions. Throughout most of the country's history, the United States was a haven for immigrants. The poem on the base of the Statue of Liberty furthers this message: "Give me your tired, your poor, [y]our huddled masses yearning to breathe free . . ."[5] By the 1920s, however, the rate of immigration from Europe and other countries had greatly slowed down. Congress passed laws to keep socialists, anarchists, and other "undesirables" out of the country. And in the South, state legislatures adopted Jim Crow laws whose goal was to keep African Americans and whites apart. African Americans were believed by some people to be inferior to whites.

Eventually, most of the eugenics laws were made illegal following World War II (1939–1945), when the truths about Nazi atrocities were revealed. The Nazis strove to develop a "master race." They applied the concept of eugenics as justification for the murders of millions of people whom they considered to be undesirables. These included Jews, gypsies, Slavs, communists, and homosexuals. To the Nazis, survival of the fittest meant killing anyone who did not fit into their concept of the master race.

Beginning in the 1950s, a series of civil rights rulings by the U.S. courts led to the end of the

Jim Crow laws. Following World War II, rules hindering the flow of immigration were eased. U.S. shores opened to a fresh wave of new citizens.

A Continued Debate

The concept of eugenics can be taken to a horrible extreme, as in the case of the Nazis and the Holocaust. After this realization, it would seem that the concept of eugenics no longer has a place in U.S. society. However, many religious leaders argue that genetic research that seeks to rid the human population of imperfections can be regarded as a form of eugenics. Few religious leaders would argue with the notion that science has the potential to eradicate disease. But they worry that experiments based on genetic science, such as stem cell research, can lead to cloning. This would be a way to create the perfect human

Hitler and Eugenics

Nazi dictator Adolf Hitler embraced the concept of eugenics, calling on the German people to destroy inferior races. He stated his philosophy in *Mein Kampf (My Struggle)*. Hitler wrote the book while in prison in 1923 and before attaining power. In *Mein Kampf*, Hitler states: "Nature . . . puts living creatures on this globe and watches the free play of forces. She then confers the master's right on her favorite child, the strongest in courage and industry. . . . The stronger must dominate and not blend with the weaker, thus sacrificing his own greatness. Only the born weakling can view this as cruel."[6]

specimen in a test tube. Christine Rosen is a staff member at the Ethics and Public Policy Center, which applies Jewish and Christian ethical arguments to public issues. Rosen says, "The question is no longer whether we will practice eugenics. We already do. The question is: Which forms of eugenics will we tolerate and how much will we allow the practice of eugenics to expand?"[7]

Embryonic stem cell research is believed to have tremendous potential for eradicating many diseases. Stem cells are the original cells that give rise to all other cells that form a human. They can divide endlessly to produce many different kinds of bodily cells. They are found in embryos, which form into babies. In stem cell therapy, stem cells are withdrawn from embryos at fertilization clinics. The embryo is destroyed in the process. Research has shown that stems cells have the potential to replace a person's damaged cells. They may be able to rid the body of disease or debilitation.

Many Catholics and other devout Christians oppose embryonic stem cell research, arguing that embryos are human lives. As evidence that all embryos can produce life, they point to the births of snowflake children. These babies were born to mothers whose embryos were preserved at the clinics through freezing, then fertilized later.

Congress has banned the use of federal funds for human cloning experiments, which has effectively stopped most human cloning research in the United States. But experimentation on animals and agricultural crops continues. In other countries, scientists are believed to be conducting human-based cloning experiments.

To many religious leaders and others, cloning experiments, stem cell research, and other genetic experiments are just a step removed from eugenics. Instead of assuring that developmentally disabled people never marry and have children, they argue, society is now on the way to creating the perfect human being in a test tube. Richard Doerflinger, associate director of Pro-Life Activities for the U.S. Conference

Eugenics Campaign in Tennessee

In 2004, the Republican candidate for Congress in Tennessee's Eighth District was James L. Hart, a vocal supporter of eugenics. Appalled by the candidate's rhetoric, Republican leaders withdrew their support for Hart even though he won the party's primary. Instead, they supported write-in candidate Dennis Bertrand. That fall, Hart and Bertrand lost to the Democratic incumbent, John Tanner.

of Catholic Bishops, says, "It's reducing human reproduction to manufacturing, completely divorced from the human relationship."[8]

The human relationship is, in part, what makes creationists so intent on having intelligent design taught in schools. Eugenics, stem cell research, and cloning deal with humans' potential ability to destroy or create life. Creationists believe that this is God's realm and not that of humans. Some creationists believe that teaching only evolution in classrooms can lead students morally and ethically astray. They believe that teaching intelligent design in classrooms would give students a moral and ethical base. ⌐

The Nazis took eugenics to the extreme and killed millions of people in an attempt to create a master race.

Members of the Kansas State Board of Education vote on the issue of evolution in Kansas public schools.

SHOULD THERE EVEN BE A DEBATE?

As the Dover case was heading to trial in late 2005, the Kansas State Board of Education adopted new principles that questioned evolution. The board encouraged students to seek "more adequate explanations of natural phenomena" in their classrooms.[1] The board's principles did not specifically recommend intelligent design as one of those "more adequate explanations." Nevertheless, supporters of evolutionary science saw the implications of the new policy and quickly raised their voices in protest. "This action is likely to be the playbook for creationism for the next several years," said Eugenie Scott. "We can predict this fight happening elsewhere."[2]

What many scientists and others who support evolutionary science find particularly frustrating is that the evolutionary model has been tested and affirmed for 150 years. Yet, they are continually called on to defend what they regard as a legitimate science. They argue that physics professors need not justify teaching Newton's laws of motion. Chemistry teachers are given a free hand to explain how atoms bond to

Flaw in Creationism

Michael J. Behe, a biologist at Lehigh University in Bethlehem, Pennsylvania, is a proponent for teaching intelligent design in public schools. However, Behe, author of the 1996 book *Darwin's Black Box*, admits that there is one fundamental flaw in teaching intelligent design in a biology classroom. There is no way to test the theory using the standard techniques of the biologist.

form molecules. Still, biologists must continually defend evolution.

Many scientists believe this to be unnecessary. When the Kansas State Board of Education organized hearings for the evolution–creationism debate, it invited the National Center for Science Education to send a representative to argue the case for evolution. The center declined, stating that offering a voice in opposition to intelligent design would legitimize intelligent design as a science. Scott said,

> We on the science side of things [skipped] the Kansas hearings because we realized this was not a scientific exchange, it was a political show trial. We are never going to solve it by throwing science at it.[3]

The Kansas mandate did not last long. Less than a year after the directive was issued, voters ousted the board members who adopted the procreationist principles. By early 2007, the Kansas antievolution guidelines were scrapped.

When voters rejected the procreationist board members, it marked the second time in six years that creationists had suffered setbacks in Kansas. In 1999, the Kansas State Board of Education deleted most references to evolution in the standards for public school science education. The action was overturned two years later by the school board after three procreationist candidates lost their seats in an election.

CREATIONISTS FIND LITTLE SUCCESS

In the 1960s, the courts started outlawing the teaching of creation in the public schools. Since then, creationists have had little success making creation science, intelligent design, or similar theories

The Science Gap

In the 1950s, the launch of Sputnik helped show that the United States had fallen behind the Soviet Union in developing new technology. As a result, science education in U.S. schools took a new direction. Science education adopted an emphasis on natural selection in biology classes. Some 50 years later, science educators are again concerned that the United States is falling behind other countries in technological achievements. They are again blaming creationists.

Some science educators suggest that the issue regarding teaching natural selection in schools has helped stall advancements in teaching science. While other countries have moved beyond such issues, the U.S. public debate still centers on whether creationist theory has a place in the classroom. Gerry Wheeler, executive director of the National Science Teachers Association, says, "It sends a signal to other countries because they're rushing to gain scientific and technological leadership while we're getting distracted with a pseudoscience issue. If I were China, I'd be happy."[4]

Those who criticize teaching creationism in the public schools point to advances in genetic science and stem cell research that have been achieved in South Korea. In the United States, both areas of study have been slowed by the refusal of the federal government to provide funding for research.

Kansas Earned an F

In a 2000 report titled "Good Science, Bad Science: Teaching Evolution in the States," Kansas received an F. This came after the Kansas State Board of Education deleted most mentions of evolution from the science curriculum in public schools. Only 24 states received an A or B from the foundation for doing a good job of teaching natural selection. A year after the report was issued, Kansas voters ousted pro-creationist school board members. Evolution was returned to the state science curriculum. Other states that received failing grades on how they teach evolution were Arkansas, Florida, Georgia, Mississippi, New Hampshire, New Mexico, North Dakota, Oklahoma, Tennessee, West Virginia, and Wyoming.

a part of the biology curriculum in public schools. Many court rulings have affirmed the separation of church and state doctrine of the U.S. Constitution. In addition, the political argument seems to have failed to gain much momentum, as shown by results of the elections in Pennsylvania, Kansas, and elsewhere.

In 2007, Republican candidates for president participating in a debate were asked to raise their hands if they did not believe in evolution. Three candidates raised their hands. One of the candidates, former Arkansas governor Mike Huckabee, said, "If you want to believe that you and your family came from apes, that's fine. I'll accept that. I just don't happen to think that I did."[5] During the presidential campaign, Huckabee endorsed teaching intelligent design and other alternative theories in public schools. Later, Huckabee went on to win primaries and caucuses in seven states before dropping out.

Lawmakers and a majority of voters seem to have little interest in ensuring that creation is taught in public school biology. So, why does the debate continue?

It might be said that one theory addresses science and the other spirituality, and that the two areas are separate issues. Evolution may be scientifically supported, but that may not stop many from believing in creationism because it does not address creationists' concerns. Evolution explains *how* life came to exist. But some creationists don't feel this is enough; their beliefs may explain *why* life exists.

Maintaining a Public Dialogue

U.S. citizens may hold strong opinions on both sides of the argument, but they also believe in fairness. Each side should be given an opportunity to make its case. John C. Green is an official of the Pew Foundation, a nonprofit

Why Brownback Raised His Hand

In 2007, Republican presidential candidate Senator Sam Brownback of Kansas raised his hand during a debate to show he did not believe in evolution. Brownback said, "Biologists will have their debates about man's origins, but people of faith can also bring a great deal to the table. For this reason, I oppose the exclusion of either faith or reason from the discussion. An attempt by either to seek a monopoly on these questions would be wrong-headed. As science continues to explore the details of man's origin, faith can do its part as well. The fundamental question for me is how these theories affect our understanding of the human person."[6]

Some students would welcome the evolution-creationism debate in a classroom setting.

organization that researches public policy topics. Green said,

> It's like they're saying, "Some people see it this way, some see it that way, so just teach it all and let the kids figure it out." It seems like a nice compromise, but it infuriates both the creationists and the scientists.[7]

Proponents of creationism strive to maintain a public dialogue. They occasionally do find ways to accomplish their goals. In 2008, the Florida Board of Education passed new guidelines for the teaching of evolution. The board did not require that intelligent design or other creationist theories be taught in the schools. Yet, it did specify that teachers must introduce evolution to their students as a "theory." Backers of evolution once more contended that while evolution is a theory, it has never failed against testing.

Finally, in 2008, the documentary *Expelled: No Intelligence Allowed* was released in theaters to a wide audience. Featuring humorist and former White House speechwriter Ben Stein, the documentary suggests that the scientific community is close-minded when it comes to teaching alternative theories. It makes the case that scientists who favor the teaching of intelligent design and similar theories are ostracized by their peers, fired from their jobs, and blacklisted from finding research jobs elsewhere. The film's producer, A. Logan Craft, said,

> We think the discussion around the origin and development of life needs a fuller play than being locked down into a Darwinian orthodoxy. . . . We're advocates for freedom of inquiry. I want to know more about intelligent design.[8]

There is a continual emergence of procreationist candidates such as Huckabee and the insistence of states such as Kansas and Florida to revisit the issue. Poll results show that U.S. citizens want to be fair. Films such as *Expelled* rekindled the issue. The evolution-creationism debate continues. ⌐

*Former Republican candidate for president Mike Huckabee
is an advocate of creationist theory.*

*Many people find a balance between
creationist and evolutionary theories.*

BELIEF IN GOD AND
EVOLUTION

n interesting point in the debate
between creationists and evolutionists
is that a significant number of eminent scientists
are deeply religious people. Yet, they are steadfast

defenders of natural selection. Likewise, many religious leaders have accepted Darwinism as a fact. But their belief in God or in the hand of a creator in the evolution of species has not lessened.

Although many creationists do not completely support the science of natural selection, some have made room in their beliefs for the basic principles of evolution. In the final analysis, intelligent design, theistic evolution, and creation science all accept to some degree the science of evolution. Each of these suggests the concepts of evolution and creationism may be compatible. The National Academy of Sciences states in its 2008 book, *Science, Evolution and Creationism*, that

> *Newspaper and television stories sometimes make it seem as though evolution and religion are incompatible, but that is not true. Many scientists and theologians have written about how one can accept both faith and validation of biological evolution. Many past and current scientists who have made major contributions to our understanding of the world have been devoutly religious. At the same time, many religious people accept the reality of evolution, and many religious denominations have issued emphatic statements reflecting this acceptance.[1]*

Oxford University Professor Richard Dawkins, author of *The God Delusion*, maintains that scientists who let their faith in God guide their judgment risk losing the burning desire to get to the truth. Dawkins says, "If ever there was a slamming of the door in the face of constructive investigation, it is the word miracle. To a medieval peasant, a radio would have seemed like a miracle. All kinds of things may happen which we by the lights of today's science would classify as a miracle just as medieval science might a Boeing 747. . . . Once you buy into the position of faith, then suddenly you find yourself losing all your natural skepticism and your scientific—really scientific—credibility."[3]

More than a Hypothesis

When Darwin first published his research, many leaders of the clergy criticized his findings. Some religious leaders in the United States, however, defended Darwin and accepted natural selection as fact. The Reverend Henry Ward Beecher, perhaps the most influential American minister during Darwin's life, embraced evolution wholeheartedly. "I am perfectly willing that it should be true, that millions of years ago, my ancestors sprang from monkeys," Beecher said.[2]

Contemporary religious leaders have also found creationism and evolution compatible. In 1950, Pope Pius XII issued an encyclical in which he found no conflict between evolution and Catholic doctrine.

Forty-six years later, Pope John Paul II further embraced Darwinism. He said, "Fresh knowledge leads to recognition of the theory of evolution as more than just a hypothesis."[4] Pope John Paul said

Henry Ward Beecher was a reverend who accepted evolutionary theory.

he was impressed by the overwhelming amount of scientific evidence supporting natural selection in the years since Darwin first published his findings.

But just because the pope found a way to accept natural selection did not mean he expelled God from the process. After endorsing natural selection, Pope John Paul insisted that the soul of every living person owes its existence to the creator. Pope John

The Vatican Observatory

In the sixteenth century, Italian astronomer Galileo made many important astronomical discoveries. He was first to observe sunspots and the moons of Jupiter. But when he suggested Earth is not at the center of the universe, he was placed under house arrest. A papal order prohibited the advancement of such theories.

Today, the Vatican has a much different attitude toward science. The institution maintains an observatory that is engaged in astronomical research. Vatican leaders see no conflict in using the power of the church to help answer scientific questions. In 2008, the Vatican Observatory took another pro-science position when it acknowledged that life on other planets is possible.

Paul said, "If the human body has its origin in living material which pre-exists it, the spiritual soul is immediately created by God."[5]

To Catholics in the United States, Pope John Paul's comments added weight to the personal beliefs of many Catholics. By the time John Paul issued his comments endorsing Darwinism, natural selection had been a part of the biology curriculum in U.S. Catholic schools for years. While some U.S. public schools wrestled with the issue of whether to teach Darwinism, Catholic students were taught the theory of natural selection straight from their biology teachers, many of whom were priests.

GENESIS IS NOT A SCIENCE TEXTBOOK

Leaders of the scientific community welcomed Pope John Paul's remarks. They believed that it showed the head of the Catholic

Church was willing to align the church's beliefs with the realities of science. They felt it was a far different attitude from that of the creationists who attempt to alter science to fit their religious beliefs.

There is no question that many of the most eminent U.S. scientists take their religion very seriously. These scientists have long been troubled by the creationists' attempts to force their ideology into high school biology classes. Francis Collins, for example, is one of the world's leading authorities on the science of genetics. He believes that God activated evolution and occupies the souls of all living creatures. But he also believes species evolved according to the framework described in *On the Origin of the Species*. Collins says,

> *There are sincere believers who interpret Genesis . . . in a very literal way that is inconsistent, frankly, with our knowledge*

Pierre Teilhard de Chardin

Pierre Teilhard de Chardin was a paleontologist and member of the team that discovered "Peking Man." The fossil of a human ancestor was found in China in the 1920s and believed to be 500,000 years old. He is also the author of *The Phenomenon of Man*, which rejected a strict interpretation of Genesis as the story behind the creation of the universe. A Catholic priest, Teilhard was a major force behind the Catholic church accepting Darwinism.

of the universe's age or how living organisms are related to each other. St. Augustine wrote that basically it is not possible to understand what was being described in Genesis. It was not intended as a science textbook. It was intended as a description of who God was, who we are and what our relationship is supposed to be with God. Augustine explicitly warns against a very narrow perspective that will put our faith at risk of looking ridiculous.[6]

Other scientists share Collins's ideas, but have had a far more difficult time finding acceptance for their viewpoints. In 2004, Olivet Nazarene University biology professor Richard Colling published a book titled *Random Designer*. He suggested that God is the force that harnessed Darwinism. Colling told his students, "I want you to know the truth that God is bigger, far more profound and vastly more creative than you may have known."[7] While it may have seemed to Colling that he had reconciled conservative religious thought with scientific fact, college administrators did not agree. Since publication of the book, Colling has been prohibited from teaching general biology classes at the Illinois university. The evangelical Church of the Nazarene sponsors the university. In addition, university administrators have told other biology teachers that they are not to use Colling's book in their classrooms.

GUIDING NATURE

Clearly, the Church of the Nazarene is not ready to accept Darwinism, even a version that is guided by the hand of God, as Colling proposed. But other religious institutions in U.S. society have accepted the challenge of defining God's role in the evolution of species. Many religious organizations have also determined

Francis Collins

Geneticist Francis Collins believes scientists are partly to blame for alienating religious people and causing much of the friction that is present in the evolution-creationism debate. Collins wrote the book *The Language of God: A Scientist Presents Evidence for Belief.* He is also head of research at the National Human Genome Research Institute, which is part of the National Institutes of Health. The mission of the institute is to identify genes that may cause disease.

Collins maintains that too many scientists have embraced the notion that a spiritual influence has no place in true science. He says,

I don't think it's fair to blame believers for getting defensive about attacks on the Bible when they see their whole belief system is under attack from some members of the scientific community who are using the platform of science to say, "We don't need God anymore, that was all superstition, and you guys should get over it." Believers then feel some requirement to respond, and this has led to an unfortunate escalation of charges and countercharges. As a result of the tensions over evolution, I think we see an increasing tendency for believers to dig in about things like Genesis . . . claiming that there is just one acceptable interpretation. That's not a strong position.[8]

Science Should Stay Out of Religion

Many scientists believe that creationism is religious doctrine that has no place in the biology classroom. Similarly, they oppose the introduction of scientific principles as part of a Sunday sermon.

The National Academy of Sciences states, "Science can neither prove nor disprove religion. Scientific advances have called some religious beliefs into question, such as the ideas that Earth was created very recently, that the sun goes around Earth, and that mental illness is due to possession by spirits or demons. But many religious beliefs involve entities or ideas that currently are not within the domain of science. Thus, it would be false to assume that all religious beliefs can be challenged by scientific findings."[10]

that it is not the role of the public schools to help define God's role. A statement by the Berkeley, California-based Center for Theology and the Natural Sciences, said, "We [cannot] allow science and religion to be seen as adversaries, for they will be locked in a conflict of mutual conquest."[9]

Religious and nonreligious people have taken both sides of the creationism-evolution argument. While much of the debate ends with personal beliefs and choices, there is still a public policy question to answer. Should intelligent design be taught in schools? History shows that each time schools say yes, the courts overturn the decision. But, more than likely, the question will continue to be debated. ⌒

Pope Pius XII believed that evolution and Catholic doctrine
could exist side by side.

TIMELINE

1800

Jean-Baptiste Antoine de Monet, also known as the Chevalier de Lamarck, first lectures that species change over time.

1831

Charles Darwin joins a scientific expedition aboard the HMS *Beagle*, which sails on December 27.

1859

On November 22, Darwin's book *On the Origin of the Species* is released.

1879

The term "social Darwinism" is first used by Oscar Schmidt in an article published in *Popular Science*.

1921

The American Eugenics Society is founded to promote the concept of genetically perfect humans.

1925

John T. Scopes is brought to trial for teaching natural selection in a Tennessee public school classroom.

1864

Herbert Spencer uses the phrase "survival of the fittest." This first suggests the concept of social Darwinism.

1869

Francis Galton advances the concept of eugenics in *Hereditary Genius.*

1871

Darwin publishes *The Descent of Man,* in which he writes about human ancestors.

1927

The U.S. Supreme Court upholds Virginia's eugenics law that the state has the right to sterilize mentally incompetent people.

1937

Biologist Theodosius Dobzhansky develops the synthetic theory of evolution that suggests species evolve over long periods of time.

1950

On August 12, Pope Pius XII issues an encyclical finding no conflict between evolution and Catholic doctrine.

TIMELINE

1957	1965	1972
Sputnik is launched on October 4; U.S. leaders realize the nation has lost its scientific edge to the Soviet Union.	Susan Epperson sues Arkansas, contending that the state's law banning the teaching of natural selection violates her right to free speech.	Paleontologists Gould and Eldredge suggest that periods of evolutionary stability are interrupted by sudden changes in species.

1996	1999	2000
On October 23, Pope John Paul II endorses natural selection, stating that evolution "is more than just a hypothesis."	The Kansas State Board of Education strikes most references to evolution from the science curricula of its schools.	The Thomas B. Fordham Foundation gives 12 states failing grades for how they teach evolution.

1973

1974

1982

Peter and Rosemary Grant begin their research on finches in the Galápagos Islands.

Three-million-year old transitional fossil, Lucy, is discovered in Ethiopia.

Equal time laws that mandate creationism be taught alongside evolution are ruled unconstitutional.

2004

2005

2008

The Dover Area School Board votes to mandate the teaching of intelligent design in ninth-grade science classes.

The Kansas State Board of Education requires science teachers to offer alternative theories to evolution.

The Florida Board of Education adopts new guidelines for science teachers requiring evolution to be identified as a "theory."

ESSENTIAL FACTS

AT ISSUE

In Favor of Teaching Intelligent Design

❖ Creationist theories provide alternative explanations for life on Earth.

❖ Creationists insist that natural selection is no more than a theory.

❖ Natural selection is an imperfect science with many questions that science has yet to explain.

❖ Scientists have uncovered no legitimate transitional fossils.

Opposed to Teaching Intelligent Design

❖ The separation of church and state doctrine of the U.S. Constitution prohibits the teaching of religious beliefs in public schools.

❖ Natural selection is proven science that has been tested and affirmed numerous times in the 150 years since Charles Darwin first published *On the Origin of the Species*.

❖ While there are many competing theories on the specifics of evolution, the general framework of the evolutionary model is irrefutable.

❖ Transitional fossils have been unearthed, particularly the fossil of "Lucy," the 3-million-year-old ancestor whose skull resembles that of an ape, but whose knees indicate she walked on two feet like a human.

CRITICAL DATES

November 22, 1859
Charles Darwin published *On the Origin of the Species*, which states that all plants and animals on Earth evolved from a single, common ancestor.

July 21, 1925
Science teacher John T. Scopes was convicted of violating the Butler Act, which banned the teaching of natural selection in Tennessee's public schools. Scopes's conviction was overturned on appeal. However, the court failed to address the issue of whether Darwinism is legitimate science.

November 12, 1968
In *Epperson v. Arkansas*, the U.S. Supreme Court overturned Arkansas's law banning the teaching of natural selection. The court declared the debate between evolution and creationism a First Amendment issue, setting a precedent that has not been overturned.

December 20, 2005
U.S. District Judge John E. Jones III ruled the Dover, Pennsylvania, intelligent design mandate was in violation of the separation of church and state provisions of the Constitution, finding that there is no scientific basis to intelligent design.

Quotes

In Favor
"The appearance of design in aspects of biology is overwhelming. . . . A reasonable person might wonder if [Darwin's] theory was missing a large piece of the puzzle."—*Biochemistry professor and author Michael J. Behe*

Opposed
"The goal of the intelligent design movement is not to encourage critical thought but to [foster] a revolution which would supplant evolutionary theory with intelligent design."—*U.S. District Judge John E. Jones III*

ADDITIONAL RESOURCES

SELECT BIBLIOGRAPHY

Blumenthal, Ralph. "In Kansas, Evolution's Backers Are Mounting a Counterattack." *New York Times*. 1 Aug. 2006.

Darwin, Charles. *On the Origin of the Species: A Facsimile of the First Edition*. Cambridge, MA: Harvard University Press, 1964.

Desmond, Adrian, and James Moore. *Darwin: The Life of a Tormented Evolutionist*. New York: Warner Books, 1991.

Scott, Eugenie C. *Evolution vs. Creationism: An Introduction*. Berkeley, CA: University of California Press, 2004.

Van Biema, David. "God vs. Science." *Time*. 13 Nov. 2006. 48.

FURTHER READING

Braun, Eric, ed. *At Issue: Creationism vs. Evolution*. San Diego, CA: Greenhaven Press, 2005.

Mautner, Stephen, ed. *Science, Evolution and Creationism*. Washington DC: National Academies Press, 2008.

Nardo, Don, ed. *Evolution*. San Diego, CA: Greenhaven Press, 2005.

WEB LINKS

To learn more about teaching intelligent design, visit ABDO Group online at **www.abdopublishing.com**. Web sites about teaching intelligent design are featured on our Book Links page. These links are routinely monitored and updated to provide the most current information available.

For More Information

For more information on this subject, contact or visit the following organizations.

American Museum of Natural History
Central Park West at Seventy-ninth Street, New York, NY 10024
212-769-5100
www.amnh.org
The museum features exhibits on natural selection, including a display on the fossil Lucy, the 3-million-year-old human ancestor. The museum's IMAX Theater features films on evolution, dinosaurs, and the origins of the universe.

Creation Museum
2800 Bullittsburg Church Road, Petersburg, KY 41080
888-582-4253
www.creationmuseum.org
The Creation Museum features exhibits that promote alternative theories to natural selection, including intelligent design, creation science, and flood geology. Visitors can examine scenes of cave dwellers mingling with dinosaurs as well as a depiction of the Garden of Eden.

National Constitution Center
Independence Mall, 525 Arch Street, Philadelphia, PA 19106
215-409-6600
www.constitutioncenter.org
Dedicated to the history of the U.S. Constitution and its application to U.S. society, this museum features many interactive exhibits that help explain the Constitution's provisions, including the separation of church and state doctrine.

GLOSSARY

big bang
> The theory that suggests the universe began 14 billion years ago during a single, cataclysmic event.

cloning
> Using artificial means to separate a cell into two or more new cells to identically reproduce an organism.

creation science
> An attempt by creationists to apply scientific principles to creationist beliefs.

creationist
> An individual who does not accept, in full or part, the framework of natural selection and believes that a divine creator has a hand in evolution.

curriculum
> All courses of study offered at a school or a college.

DNA
> Deoxyribonucleic acid; found in the nuclei of all cells, DNA is the chemical that transmits hereditary characteristics from one generation to the next.

eugenics
> A concept that deals with the improvement of the human race through genetics.

evolution
> The scientific process in which species continually change and adapt to their environments over time.

flood geology
> The belief that suggests mountains, valleys, and other geological characteristics of the Earth formed as the waters of the Great Flood receded.

fundamentalist
> A person who maintains a literal interpretation of the Bible, believing every word is factually true.

Genesis

First book of the Old Testament in which God is said to have created Earth in six days and species separately.

intelligent design

The creationist belief that suggests life forms are too complicated to have evolved entirely through natural selection, and, therefore, the hand of an "intelligent designer" is also responsible for evolution.

natural selection

A scientific principle that states all living things have evolved from a single, common ancestor.

old earth creationism

A creationist view that accepts the scientific explanation for the age of Earth but holds that life was created relatively recently.

paleontologist

A scientist who explores extinct life forms, often by studying fossils or other evidence left behind from earlier ages.

Quran

The sacred scriptures of the Islamic religion containing revelations made to the Prophet Muhammad by God.

separation of church and state

Basic right guaranteed by the U.S. Constitution to guard against the establishment of a state religion.

stem cell research

Medical research that seeks to cure disease by replacing diseased or damaged cells with cells withdrawn from embryonic stem cells.

theistic evolution

Creationist doctrine that accepts the scientific explanation for evolution but believes life has evolved according to a divine plan.

young earth creationism

A literal interpretation of Genesis suggesting that Earth is between 6,000 and 10,000 years old.

SOURCE NOTES

Chapter 1. The Dover Case

1. Francisco J. Ayala. *Darwin's Gift to Science and Religion*. Washington DC: Joseph Henry Press, 2007. 170.
2. Ibid.
3. Percival Davis and Dean H. Kenyon. *Of Pandas and People: The Central Question of Biological Origins*. Dallas: Haughton, 2005. 99–100.
4. Laurie Goodstein. "A Web of Faith, Law and Science in Evolution Suit." *New York Times*. 26 Sept. 2005: A-1.
5. "Judgment Day: Intelligent Design on Trial." *NOVA*, 13 Nov. 2007. 22 July 2008 <http://www.pbs.org/wgbh/nova/transcripts/3416_id.html>.
6. Peter Baker and Peter Slevin. "Bush Remarks on 'Intelligent Design' Theory Fuel Debate." *Washington Post*: 3 Aug. 2005: A-1.
7. Ibid.
8. Sean Cavanagh. "Defense Gets Its Days in Court in Support of 'Intelligent Design.'" *Education Week*. 26 Oct. 2005: 6.
9. "Judgment Day: Intelligent Design on Trial." *NOVA*, 13 Nov. 2007. 22 July 2008 <http://www.pbs.org/wgbh/nova/id/judge.html>.

Chapter 2. Charles Darwin and Natural Selection

1. Charles Hodge. "What is Darwinism?" *Project Gutenberg*. 22 July 2008 <http://www.gutenberg.org/ebooks/19192>.
2. Adrian Desmond and James Moore. *Darwin: The Life of a Tormented Evolutionist*. New York: Warner Books, 1991. 477.
3. Leonard Huxley and Thomas Henry Huxley. *Life and Letters of Thomas Henry Huxley*. New York: D. Appleton, 1900. 201.
4. Adrian Desmond and James Moore. *Darwin: The Life of a Tormented Evolutionist*. New York: Warner Books, 1991. 496.
5. David N. Livingstone. *Darwin's Forgotten Defenders*. Vancouver, BC: Regent College Publishers, 1984. 42.
6. Charles Darwin. *On the Origin of the Species: A Facsimile of the First Edition*. Cambridge, MA: Harvard University Press, 1964. 351.
7. "Darwin's Predictions," Judgment Day: Intelligent Design on Trial. *NOVA*. 13 Nov. 2007. 22 July 2008 <http://www.pbs.org/wgbh/nova/id/pred-nf.html>.
8. Rick Weiss. "New Clue May Link Dinosaurs to Birds." *Pittsburgh Post-Gazette*. 25 Apr. 2007. A-2.

Chapter 3. Creationist Beliefs

1. Gen. 1:25–27 Authorized (King James) Version.
2. Eugenie C. Scott. Evolution vs. Creationism: An Introduction. Berkeley, CA: University of California Press, 2004. 52.

3. "An Affirmation of Creation." Seventh-Day Adventist Church. 22 July 2008 <http://www.adventist.org/beliefs/statements/main_stat54.html>.

4. Benjamin McArthur. "The New Creationists." *American Heritage*. Nov. 1994. 106.

5. "Judgment Day: Intelligent Design on Trial." *NOVA*. 13 Nov. 2007. 22 July 2008 <http://www.pbs.org/wgbh/nova/id/defense-id.html>.

6. Ibid.

Chapter 4. Evolution of the Debate

1. "Sunday Hits Darwin for Nature Faking." *New York Times* Online. 25 May 1917. 28 July 2008 <http://query.nytimes.com/mem/archive-free/pdf?_r=1&res=9C06E2D8123AE433A25756C2A9639C946696D6CF&oref=slogin>.

2. Richard Milner. *The Encyclopedia of Evolution*. New York: Facts on File, 1990. 64.

3. Ibid. 397.

4. Stephen Mautner, ed. *Science, Evolution and Creationism*. Washington DC: National Academies Press, 2008. 44.

Chapter 5. An Imperfect Science

1. Gordy Slack. "The Atheist." *Salon.com*. 4 Apr. 2005. 22 July 2008 <http://dir.salon.com/story/news/feature/2005/04/30/dawkins/index.html>.

2. Henry Morris. "Evolution—A House Divided." *Institute for Creation Research*. 22 July 2008 <http://www.icr.org/articles/view/298//>.

3. John Rennie. "15 Answers to Creationist Nonsense." *Scientific American*. July 2002. 78.

4. Ibid.

5. Stephen Mautner, ed. *Science, Evolution and Creationism*. Washington DC: National Academies Press, 2008. 44.

6. Jonathan Weiner. "The Handy-Dandy Evolution Prover." *New York Times*. 8 May 1994. A-40.

7. Ibid.

8. Henry Morris. "Evolution—A House Divided." *Institute for Creation Research*. 22 July 2008 <http://www.icr.org/articles/view/298//>.

9. Henry Morris. "Geology and the Flood." *Institute for Creation Research*. 22 July 2008 <http://www.icr.org/article/54>.

10. John Rennie. "15 Answers to Creationist Nonsense." *Scientific American*. July 2002. 78.

SOURCE NOTES CONTINUED

Chapter 6. Social Darwinism
1. Gregory J. Schneider. "True Darwinists Can Be a Dangerous Lot." *Topeka Capital-Journal*. 21 Nov. 2005. 24 Nov. 2008 <http://www.cjonline. com/stories/112105/opi_darwinists.shtml>.
2. William L. Johnson. "Evolution." *Vital Speeches of the Day*. 15 Feb. 1995. 281.
3. Ted Peters and Martinez Hewlett. *Evolution from Creation to New Creation: Conflict, Conversation, and Convergence*. Nashville, TN: Abingdon Press, 2003. 54.
4. Ibid.
5. "Encyclical of Pope Leo XIII Promulgated on 15 May 1891." Eternal World Television Network. 24 Nov. 2008 <http://www.ewtn.com/library/ ENCYC/L13RERUM.HTM>.
6. Gen. 6:5–7 AV.
7. William L. Johnson. "Evolution." *Vital Speeches of the Day*. 15 Feb. 1995. "Evolution." 281.

Chapter 7. Eugenics, Stem Cell Research, and Cloning
1. Richard Milner. *The Encyclopedia of Evolution*. New York: Facts on File, 1990. 156.
2. Ted Peters and Martinez Hewlett. *Evolution from Creation to New Creation: Conflict, Conversation, and Convergence*. Nashville, TN: Abingdon Press, 2003. 56.
3. Marie McCullough. "Nobody's Perfect—But We're Still Trying." *Philadelphia Inquirer*. 27 Oct. 2003. C-1.
4. Ibid.
5. Emma Lazarus. "The New Colossus." *The Academy of American Poets*. 6 Aug. 2008 <http://www.poets.org/viewmedia.php/prmMID/16111>.
6. William L. Shirer. *The Rise and Fall of the Third Reich: The History of Nazi Germany*. New York: Simon and Schuster, 1960. 86.
7. Marie McCullough. "Nobody's Perfect—But We're Still Trying." *Philadelphia Inquirer*. 27 Oct. 2003. C-1.
8. Yonat Shimron. "Scientists, Religious Groups Grapple with Concept of Cloning." *Raleigh News and Observer*. 17 Jan. 2008.

Chapter 8. Should There Even Be a Debate?
1. Ralph Blumenthal. "In Kansas, Evolution's Backers Are Mounting a Counterattack.' *New York Times*. 1 Aug. 2006. A-1.
2. John Hanna, Associated Press. "Kansas Board Votes for ID in Schools." *Hanover Evening Sun*. 9 Nov. 2005.

3. Cornelia Dean. "Opting Out in the Debate on Evolution." *New York Times*. 21 June 2005. F-1.

4. Claudia Wallis. "Evolution Wars." *Time*. 15 Aug. 2005. 26.

5. Elizabeth Holbert. "Old Habits." *New Yorker*. 7 Jan. 2008. 29.

6. Sam Brownback. "What I Think about Evolution." *New York Times*. 31 May 2007. A-19.

7. Laurie Goodstein. "Teaching Creationism Is Endorsed in New Survey." *New York Times*. 31 Aug. 2005. A-9.

8. Cheryl Hall. "Intelligent Design Documentary Creates Stir." *Dallas Morning News*. 27 April 2008. 22 July 2008 <http://www.dallasnews.com/sharedcontent/dws/bus/columnists/chall/stories/DN-Hall_27bus.ART0.State.Edition1.4655452.html>.

Chapter 9. Belief in God and Evolution

1. Stephen Mautner, ed. *Science, Evolution and Creationism*. Washington DC: National Academies Press, 2008. 49.

2. Eleanor Kirk, ed. *Beecher as Humorist*. New York: Fords, Howard and Hulbert, 1887. 11.

3. David Van Biema. "God vs. Science." *Time*. 13 Nov. 2006. 48.

4. John Tagliabue. "Pope Bolsters Church's Support for Scientific View of Evolution." *New York Times*. 25 Oct. 1996. A-1.

5. Ibid.

6. David Van Biema. "God vs. Science." *Time*. 13 Nov. 2006. 48.

7. Sharon Begley. "Can God Love Darwin, Too?" *Newsweek*. 17 Sept. 2007. 45.

8. David Ewing Duncan. "The Discover Interview: Francis Collins." *Discover*. February 2007. 44.

9. National Center for Science Education. "Statements from Religious Organizations." 22 July 2008 <http://www.ncseweb.org/resources/articles/1028_statements_from_religious_org_12_19_2002.asp#ctns>.

10. Stephen Mautner, ed. *Science, Evolution and Creationism*. Washington DC: National Academies Press, 2008. 54.

INDEX

ABOUT THE AUTHOR

Hal Marcovitz is a former newspaper reporter who has written more than 100 books for young readers. In 2005, *Nancy Pelosi*, his biography of House Speaker Nancy Pelosi, was named to *Booklist* magazine's list of recommended feminist books for young readers. As a journalist, he won three Keystone Press Awards, the highest award for newspaper reporting presented by the Pennsylvania Newspaper Association. He lives in Pennsylvania.

PHOTO CREDITS

Robert Record/iStock Photo, cover; Bradley C. Bower/AP Images, 6; Dan Loh/AP Images, 12; Niklas Larsson/AP Images, 15; AP Images, 16, 26, 39, 43, 59, 75, 95; Isabell Christensen/AP Images, 20; Pat Sullivan/AP Images, 25; Ed Reinke/AP Images, 31; Matthias Rietschel/AP Images, 35; Francis Miller/Time & Life Pictures/Getty Images, 36; Howard Sochurek/Time & Life Pictures/Getty Images, 45; Antonin Kratochvil/AP Images, 46; Rosemary Grant/AP Images, 51; Tim Graham/Getty Images, 55; Hulton-Deutsch Collection/Corbis, 56; Jason R. Henske, 62; Janet Hostetter/AP Images, 65; Gene J. Puskar/AP Images, 66; Charlie Riedel/AP Images, 76; Don Ryan/AP Images, 82; Lynne Sladky/AP Images, 85; Justin Lane/epa/Corbis, 86; Hulton Archive/Stringer/Getty Images, 89